PIANO • VOCAL • GUITAR

ONE DIRECTION
FOUR

ISBN 978-1-4950-1210-5

HAL•LEONARD®
CORPORATION
7777 W. BLUEMOUND RD. P.O. BOX 13819 MILWAUKEE, WI 53213

For all works contained herein:
Unauthorized copying, arranging, adapting, recording, Internet posting, public performance,
or other distribution of the printed music in this publication is an infringement of copyright.
Infringers are liable under the law.

Visit Hal Leonard Online at
www.halleonard.com

CONTENTS

- 4 STEAL MY GIRL
- 9 READY TO RUN
- 18 WHERE DO BROKEN HEARTS GO
- 28 18
- 37 GIRL ALMIGHTY
- 44 FOOL'S GOLD
- 52 NIGHT CHANGES
- 59 NO CONTROL
- 66 FIREPROOF
- 71 SPACES
- 78 STOCKHOLM SYNDROME
- 84 CLOUDS

STEAL MY GIRL

Words and Music by LOUIS TOMLINSON,
LIAM PAYNE, JULIAN BUNETTA,
WAYNE HECTOR, EDWARD DREWETT
and JOHN RYAN

Moderate Rock beat

Copyright © 2014 PPM Music Ltd., Holy Cannoli Music, Warner/Chappell Music Publishing Ltd., BMG Platinum Songs, Music Of Big Deal, Bob Erotik Music and The Family Songbook
All Rights for PPM Music Ltd. in the U.S. and Canada Administered by Downtown DMP Songs
All Rights for Holy Cannoli Music Administered by Songs Of Universal, Inc.
All Rights for Warner/Chappell Music Publishing Ltd. in the U.S. and Canada Administered by Warner-Tamerlane Publishing Corp.
All Rights for BMG Platinum Songs, Music Of Big Deal, Bob Erotik Music and The Family Songbook Administered by BMG Rights Management (US) LLC
All Rights Reserved   Used by Permission

B♭
She be my queen since we were six - teen. We want the same things, we dream the same dreams, al - right.
Kiss - es like cream, her walk is so mean, and ev - 'ry jaw drop when she's in those jeans, al - right.
E♭5 E♭maj7 E♭6 E♭maj7 E♭5 E♭maj7 E♭6 E♭maj7
6fr 3fr
Al - right.
Al - right.
B♭
I got it all 'cause she is the one. Her mom calls me "love," her dad calls me "son," al - right.
I don't ex - ist if I don't have her. The sun does - n't shine, the world does - n't turn, al - right.
E♭5 E♭maj7 E♭6 E♭maj7 E♭5 E♭maj7 E♭6 E♭maj7
Al - right. I know,
Al - right. But I know,

I know, I know for sure.
I know, I know for sure.

Ev-'ry-bod-y wan-na steal my girl, ev-'ry-bod-y wan-na take her heart a-way.

Cou-ple bil-lion in the whole wide world, find an-oth-er one 'cause she be-longs to me.

Ev-'ry-bod-y wan-na steal my girl, ev-'ry-bod-y wan-na take her heart a-way.

7

never let her down before. She knows, she knows that I'm never gonna let another take her love from me, now.

CODA

Na na, she belongs to me.

Na na na na na na. Na na na na na na.

Na na na na na na. She belongs to me.

D.S. al Coda

10

| Bm7 | Gsus2 | D5/A |

I'll never make it out alive. But I know,

| Bm7 | Gsus2 | D5/A |

yes I know we'll be alright. There's a de-

| Bm7 | Gsus2 | D5 |

-vil in your smile, it's chasing me. And

| Bm7 | Gsus2 | D5 |

ev-'ry time I turn around, it's only gaining speed. There's a mo-

-ment when you fi-n'lly re-a-lize _____ there's no way _____ you can change _____ the roll-ing tide. _____ But I know, _____ yes I know _____ that I'll _____ be fine. _____

This time _____ I'm read-y _____ to run, escape from the cit - y and fol - low the sun. 'Cause I

want to be yours, don't you want to be mine? I don't

want to get lost in the dark of the night.

This time I'm read - y to run. Whereev - er __ you are is __ the place I __ be - long. 'Cause I want to be __ free __ and I want to be __ young. __ I will never look __ back, __ now __ I'm read - y __ to run. I'm read - y __ to run.

14

D5 | **Bm7** | **Gsus2**

There's a future in my life I can't foresee.

D5 | **Bm7** | **Gsus2**

Unless, of course, I stay on course and

D5 | **Bm7** | **Gsus2**

keep you next to me. There will always be the kind that criti-

D5 | **Bm7** | **Gsus2** | **D5** | **D.S. al Coda**

N.C.

cize. But I know, yes I know we'll be alright.

drum fill

CODA

read - y ____ to run.

This time ___ I'm read - y ____ to run. _____

I'd give ev - 'ry - thing that __ I've got for __ your love. _____

This time I'm ready to run, escape from the city and follow the sun. 'Cause I want to be yours, don't you want to be mine? I don't want to get lost in the dark of the night. This time I'm ready to

G
run. Where - ev - er you are is the
place I be - long. 'Cause I want to be free and I
D
G
D
G
D
want to be young. I will nev - er look back, now I'm
A
N.C.
read - y to run.

WHERE DO BROKEN HEARTS GO

Words and Music by HARRY STYLES,
JULIAN BUNETTA, RUTH ANN CUNNINGHAM,
ALEXANDRA TAMPOSI and TEGGY GEIGER

Anthemic Pop Rock

Count-ed all my mis-takes_ and there's on-ly one,_ stand-ing out from the list_ of the things_ I've done._ All the rest of my crimes_ don't come_ close to the look on your face_ when I let_ you go. So I built you a house_

Copyright © 2014 PPM Music Ltd., Holy Cannoli Music, Sony/ATV Music Publishing (UK) Limited,
Perfect Storm Music Group AB, Music Of Big Deal, TG WorldWide Publishing and The Family Songbook
All Rights for PPM Music Ltd. Administered by Downtown DMP Songs
All Rights for Holy Cannoli Music Administered by Songs Of Universal, Inc.
All Rights for Sony/ATV Music Publishing (UK) Limited and Perfect Storm Music Group AB Administered by Sony/ATV Music Publishing LLC, 424 Church Street, Suite 1200, Nashville, TN 37219
All Rights for Music Of Big Deal, TG WorldWide Publishing and The Family Songbook Administered by BMG Rights Management (US) LLC
All Rights Reserved   Used by Permission

from a broken home and I wrote you a song_ with the words_ you spoke._ Yeah, it took me some time,_ but I figured out_ how to fix up a heart that I let down._ Now, I'm searching ev-'ry lonely place. Ev-'ry corner, calling out your name. Try'n' to find_ you, but I just don't know; ___ where do broken hearts go?

Where do broken hearts go. ___ Yeah, the taste of your lips ___

___ on the tip of my tongue ___ is at the top of the list ___ of the things ___ I want. ___

___ Mind is running in cir - cles of you ___ and me, ___ an - y - one in be - tween ___

_____ is the en - e - my. Shad - ows come with the pain _____ that you're run - ning from. _____ Love was some - thing you've nev - er heard _____ e - nough. _____ Yeah, it took me some time, _____ but I fig - ured out _____ how to fix up a heart that I let down. _____

Now, I'm searching ev-'ry lone-ly place.

Ev-'ry cor-ner, call-ing out your name.

Try'n' to find you, but I just don't know;

where do bro-ken hearts go?

23

Tell me now, tell me now, tell me where you go when you feel afraid. Where do broken hearts go?

Tell me now, tell me now, tell me will you ever love me again, love me again?

D.S. al Coda

25

Tell ____ me, 'cause I'm ten feet down. ____ Where ____ do bro-ken hearts go? Come on, ba-by, come and get me out. Come on, ba-by come and get me out.

27

Come on, ba - by, 'cause I need you now.

Where do bro - ken hearts go? Where do bro - ken hearts go? Where do bro - ken hearts go?

Where do bro - ken hearts go?

18

Words and Music by ED SHEERAN and OLIVER FRANK

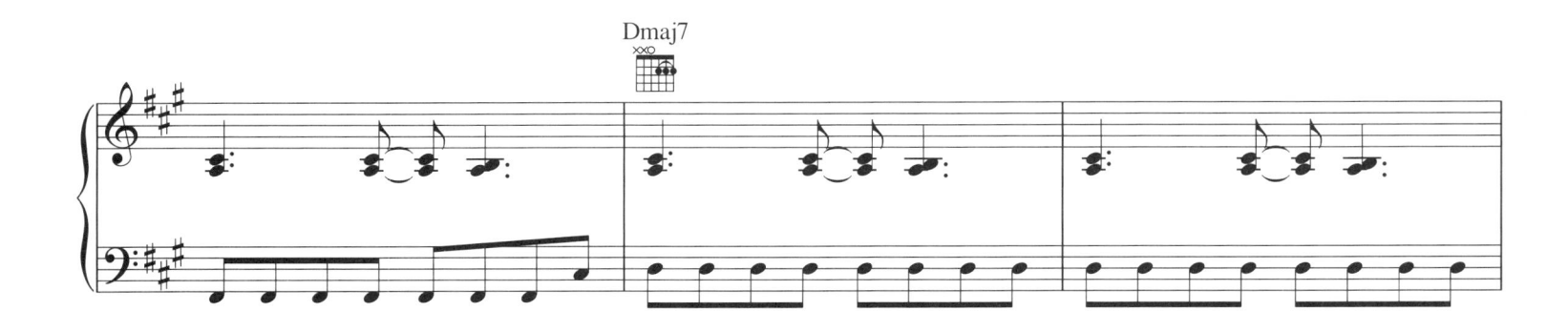

Pop Rock

I've got a heart and I've got a soul. Be-lieve

Copyright © 2014 Sony/ATV Music Publishing (UK) Limited
All Rights Administered by Sony/ATV Music Publishing LLC, 424 Church Street, Suite 1200, Nashville, TN 37219
International Copyright Secured   All Rights Reserved

me, I will use them both.

We made a start, be it a false

one, I know. Baby, I don't want

to feel alone. So

E D E
kiss me where I lay down, _ my hands pressed to your
D E D
cheeks. A long way from the play - ground.
A D F♯m
I have loved you _ since _ we were eight - een.
E A D
Long be - fore we both _ thought the same thing.

31

(Lyrics)

To be loved and to be in love. All I can do is say that these arms were made for holding you, oh. I want to love like you made me feel when we were eight-een.

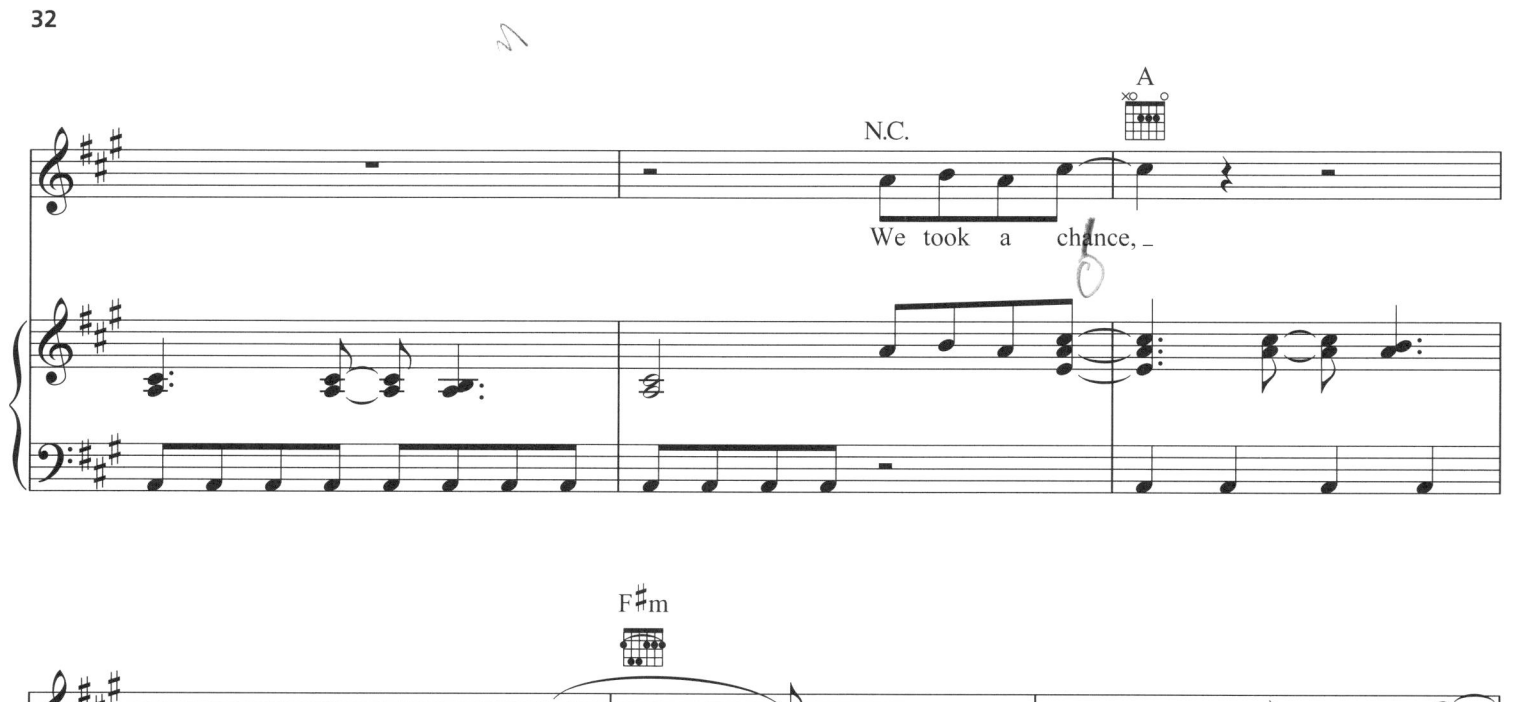

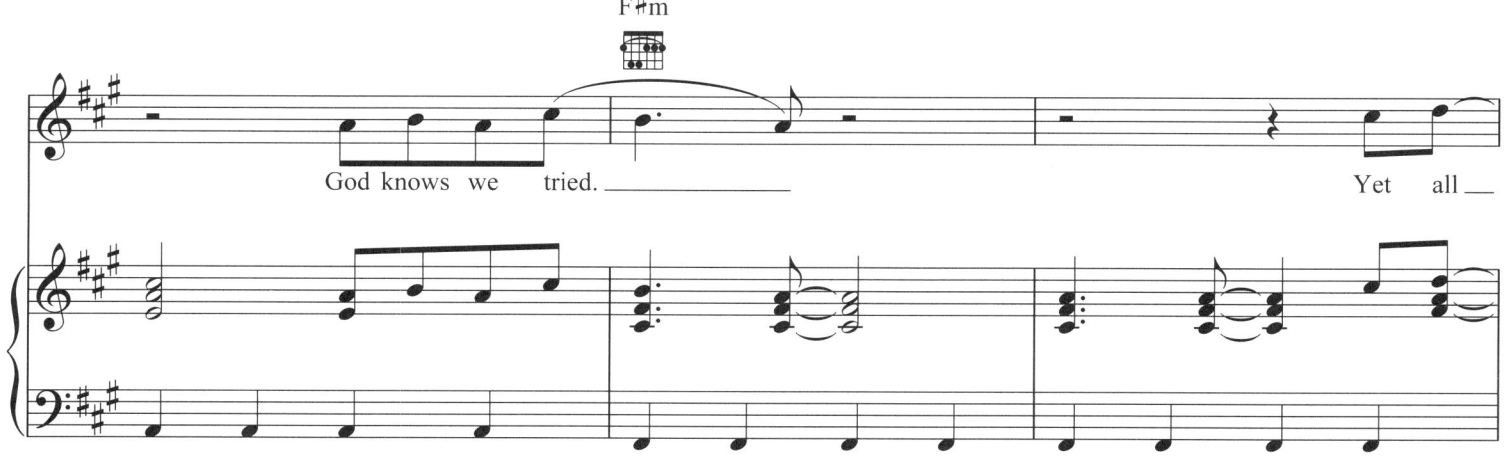

We took a chance, God knows we tried. Yet all a-long, I knew we'd be fine. So pour me a drink, oh love, let's split the night wide o-pen and we'll see ev-'ry-thing we can, live and love in slow mo-tion, mo-tion, mo-tion.

D.S. al Coda

So

CODA

we were eight-een.

When

we were eight-een. Oh, Lord, when _we were eight-een._ Kiss me where I lay down, my hands pressed to your cheeks. A long way from the play-ground. I have loved you since

35

A
D
F♯m
I want to love like you made me feel when
E
A
D
we were eight - een. I want to love like you made
F♯m
E
A
me feel when we were eight - een. I want to love
D
F♯m
E
N.C.
like you made me feel when we were eight - een.

GIRL ALMIGHTY

Words and Music by JOHN RYAN,
JULIAN BUNETTA and SCOTT MEHNER

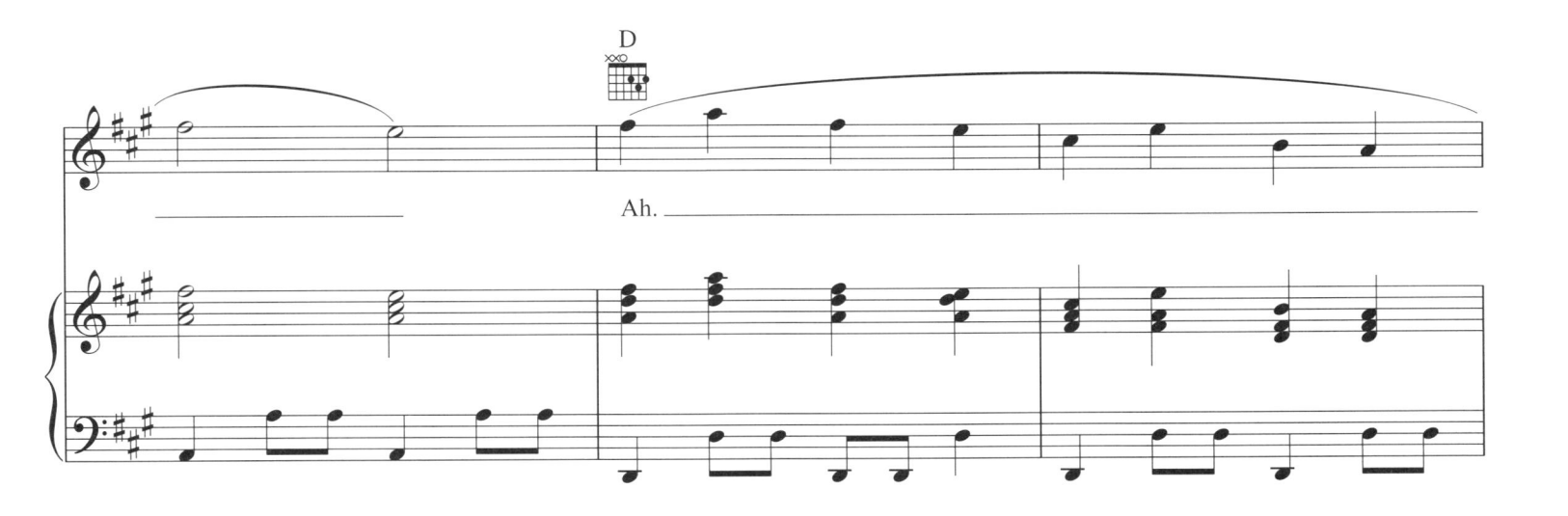

Oh, ___ no, ___ no, no. ___

Ah. ___

Her light is as loud as as man-y am-bu-lanc-es as it takes to save a sav-ior, oh. ___

Whoa, oh, oh. And while she floats through the room on a big balloon, some say, "She's such a fake," that her love is made up, no. No, no, no. Let's have another toast to the

A D E D E D
girl al - might - y. Let's
A N.C. A D E
pray we stay young, stay made of light - ning.
D E D A D
Am I the on - ly, on - ly be -
A N.C. E
liev - er? There is some - thing hap -

F♯m
D
-pen-ning here, there's some-thing hap-pen-ning here. The
A
D
A
on-ly, on-ly be-liev-er.
N.C.
E
F♯m
There is some-thing hap-pen-ing here,
D
A
I hope you feel what I'm feel-ing too.

I get down, I get down, I get down on my knees for you. Ooh. I get down, I get down, I get down on my knees. I get down on my knees for you.

Her

FOOL'S GOLD

Words and Music by LOUIS TOMLINSON,
LIAM PAYNE, NIALL HORAN,
ZAYN MALIK, HARRY STYLES,
JAMIE SCOTT and MAUREEN McDONALD

Moderate half-time feel

I'm like a crow on a wire; you're the shin-ing dis-trac-tion that makes me fly. Oh, oh, oh.

* Recorded a half step lower.

Copyright © 2014 PPM Music Ltd., EMI Music Publishing Ltd. and Jmo Zella Mo Music
All Rights for PPM Music Ltd. Administered by Downtown DMP Songs
All Rights for EMI Music Publishing Ltd., EMI April Music Inc. and Mo Zella Mo Music Administered by Sony/ATV Music Publishing LLC, 424 Church Street, Suite 1200, Nashville, TN 37219
All Rights Reserved   Used by Permission

Lyrics:
I'm like a boat on the water; you're the rays on the waves that calm my mind, oh, ev-'ry time. And I know in my heart you're

not a con-stant star. And yeah, I let you use me from the day that we first met, but I'm not done yet falling for your fool's gold. And

I knew that you turn it on for ev'ry-one you met, but I don't re-gret falling for your fool's gold.

I'm the first to admit that I'm reckless; I get lost in your beauty, and I can't see two feet in front of me. And I know in my heart, you're just a moving part. And

Oh, oh.

Yeah, I know your love's not real; that's not the way it feels. That's not the way it feels.

And yes, I let

G
Em
you use me from the day that we first met, but I'm
C
G
not done yet falling for your fool's
C
G
C
gold. And I knew that you turn it on for
G
Em
C
ev - 'ry - one you met, but I don't re - gret

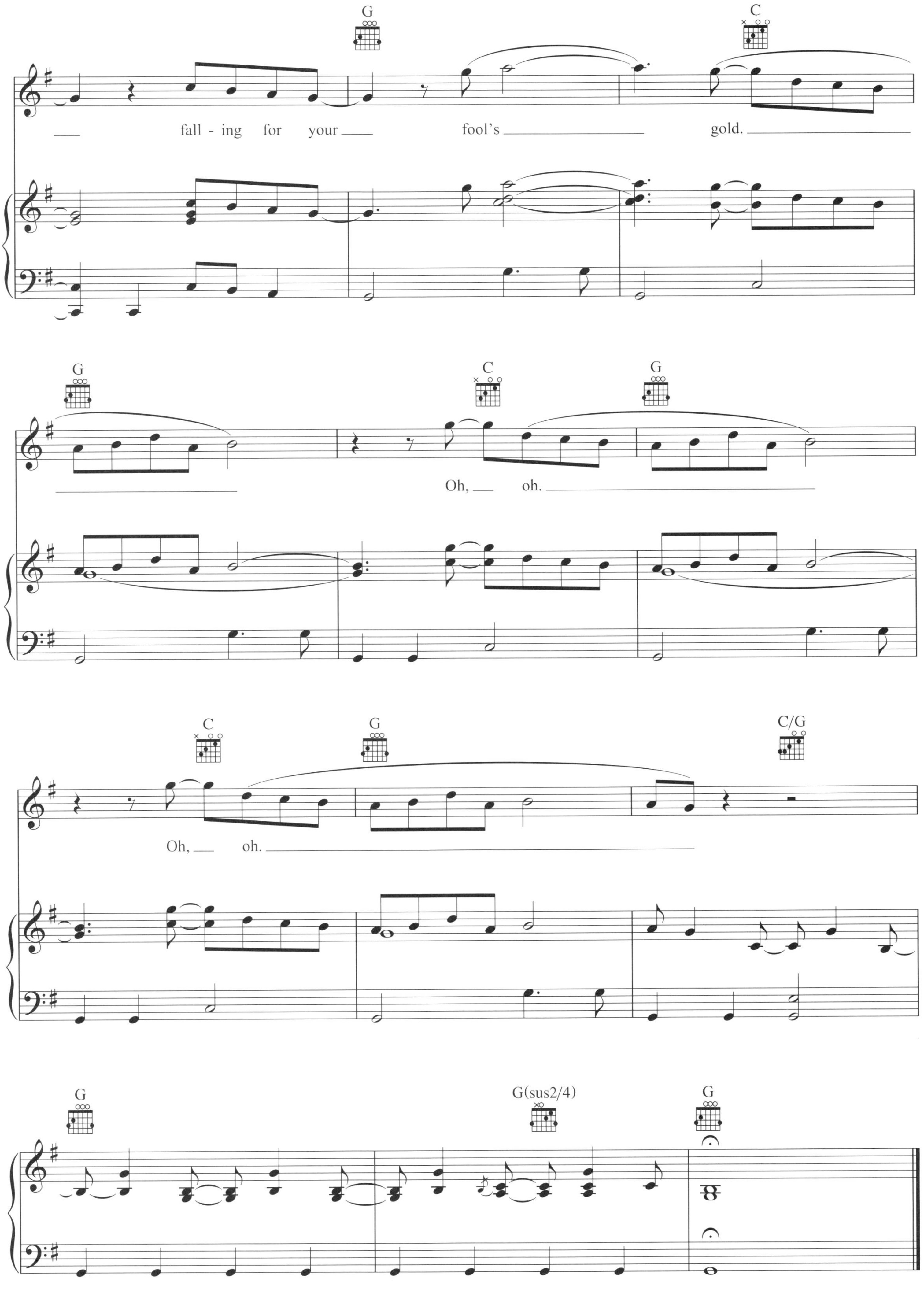
G
C
fall - ing for your fool's gold.
G
C
G
Oh, oh.
C
G
C/G
Oh, oh.
G
G(sus2/4)
G

NIGHT CHANGES

Words and Music by LOUIS TOMLINSON,
LIAM PAYNE, NIALL HORAN,
ZAYN MALIK, HARRY STYLES,
JULIAN BUNETTA, JAMIE SCOTT
and JOHN RYAN

Moderately

Going out to-night; chang-
Chas-ing it to-night; doubts

-es in-to some-thing red. Her moth-er does-n't like that kind of dress.
are run-nin' 'round her head. He's wait-ing; hides be-hind a cig-a-rette.

Ev-'ry-thing she nev-er had, she's show-ing off.
Heart is beat-in' loud, and she does-n't want it to stop.

Copyright © 2014 PPM Music Ltd., Holy Cannoli Music, EMI Music Publishing Ltd., BMG Platinum Songs, Music Of Big Deal, Bob Erotik Music and The Family Songbook
All Rights for PPM Music Ltd. Administered by Downtown DMP Songs
All Rights for Holy Cannoli Music Administered by Songs Of Universal, Inc.
All Rights for EMI Music Publishing Ltd. Administered by Sony/ATV Music Publishing LLC, 424 Church Street, Suite 1200, Nashville, TN 37219
All Rights for BMG Platinum Songs, Music Of Big Deal, Bob Erotik Music and The Family Songbook Administered by BMG Rights Management (US) LLC
All Rights Reserved   Used by Permission

E♭sus
A♭
Driv-ing too fast; moon
Mov-ing too fast; moon
Fm7
is break-ing through her hair. She's head-ing for some-
is light-ing up her skin. She's fall-ing, does-
Cm(add♭6)
thing that she won't for-get.
n't e-ven know it yet.
Hav-ing no re-grets is all
E♭sus
that she real-ly wants.

We're only getting older, baby, and I've been thinking about it lately: does it ever drive you crazy, just how fast the night changes, ev'rything that you've ever dreamed of disappearing when you wake up?

But there's noth-ing to be a-fraid of; e-ven when the night chang-es, it will nev-er change me and you. chang-es, it will nev-er change me and you.

Gm7
E♭(add2)
6fr
Fsus
B♭
Go - ing out to - night; chang - es in - to some-thing red.
Gm7
Her moth - er does - n't like that kind of dress; re -
Dm
F6
minds her of the miss - ing piece of in - no - cence she lost.

We're only getting older, baby, and I've been thinking about it lately: does it ever drive you crazy, just how fast the night changes, ev'rything that you've ever dreamed of disappearing when you wake up?

But there's noth-ing to be a-fraid of; e-ven when the night chang-es, it will nev-er change, ba-by, it will nev-er change, ba-by, it will nev-er change me and you.

NO CONTROL

Words and Music by LOUIS TOMLINSON,
LIAM PAYNE, JULIAN BUNETTA,
JAMIE SCOTT, RUTH ANN CUNNINGHAM
and JOHN RYAN

-ger-print of lip-stick's not e-nough.
-na wash a-way the night be-fore.

Sweet
In the heat

where you lay; still a trace
where you lay, I could stay

of in-no-cence on the pil-low-case.
right here and burn in it all day.

Waking up beside you, I'm a loaded gun. I can't contain this anymore. I'm all yours; I've got no control, no control. Powerless, and I don't care. It's ob - vi - ous, I just can't get e - nough of you. The ped - al's down, my eyes are closed; no con - trol.

(Oh.) Whoa.

(Oh.) Taste No con - trol. Lost

my sens - es, I'm de - fens - less. Her per - fume's hold - ing me ran - som. Sweet and so - ur, heart de - vour - ed. Ly - ing here, I count the ho - urs. Wak - ing up be - side you, I'm a load - ed gun. I can't con - tain this *any-more. I'm all yours; I've got no con-trol, no con-trol. Pow-er-less, and I don't care. It's ob-vi-ous, I just can't get e-nough of you. The ped-al's down, my eyes are closed; no con-trol.*

Whoa.

No con-trol. Pow-er-less, and I don't care. It's ob-vi-ous, I just can't get e-nough of you. The ped-al's down, my eyes are closed; no con-trol.

FIREPROOF

Words and Music by LOUIS TOMLINSON, LIAM PAYNE, JULIAN BUNETTA, JAMIE SCOTT and JOHN RYAN

Moderate Pop

I think I'm gonna lose my mind.
I'm feelin' somethin' deep inside.

Somethin' deep inside me, I can't give up. ____ I think I'm gonna
Hotter than a jet stream, burnin' up. ____ I got a feelin'

lose my mind. I roll ____ and I roll ____ 'til I'm out ____ of luck. ____ Yeah, I roll ____
deep inside. It's taken, it's taken ____ all ____ I've got. ____ Yeah, it's tak-

Copyright © 2014 PPM Music Ltd., Holy Cannoli Music, EMI Music Publishing Ltd., BMG Platinum Songs, Music Of Big Deal, Bob Erotik Music and The Family Songbook
All Rights for PPM Music Ltd. Administered by Downtown DMP Songs
All Rights for Holy Cannoli Music Administered by Songs Of Universal, Inc.
All Rights for EMI Music Publishing Ltd. Administered by Sony/ATV Music Publishing LLC, 424 Church Street, Suite 1200, Nashville, TN 37219
All Rights for BMG Platinum Songs, Music Of Big Deal, Bob Erotik Music and The Family Songbook Administered by BMG Rights Management (US) LLC
All Rights Reserved   Used by Permission

and I roll 'til I'm out of luck.
-en, it's tak-en all I've got. 'Cause no-bod-y knows

you, ba-by, the way I do. And no-bod-y loves

you, ba-by, the way I do. It's been so long.

It's been so long. May-be you are fire-proof.

'Cause no-bod-y sends me, ba-by, the way you do.

I think I'm gon-na win this time. Rid-in' on the wind and I won't give up. I think I'm gon-na win this time. I roll and I roll 'til I change my luck. Yeah, I roll and I roll 'til I change

_____ my luck. _____

'Cause no-bod-y knows _____ you, ba-by, the way I _____ do. _____ And no-bod-y loves _____ you, ba-by, the way I do. It's been so long. It's been so long.

You must be fire-proof.
Maybe you are fire-proof.
'Cause nobody sends me, baby, the way you do.

SPACES

Words and Music by LOUIS TOMLINSON, LIAM PAYNE, JULIAN BUNETTA, JAMIE SCOTT and JOHN RYAN

Moderately slow groove

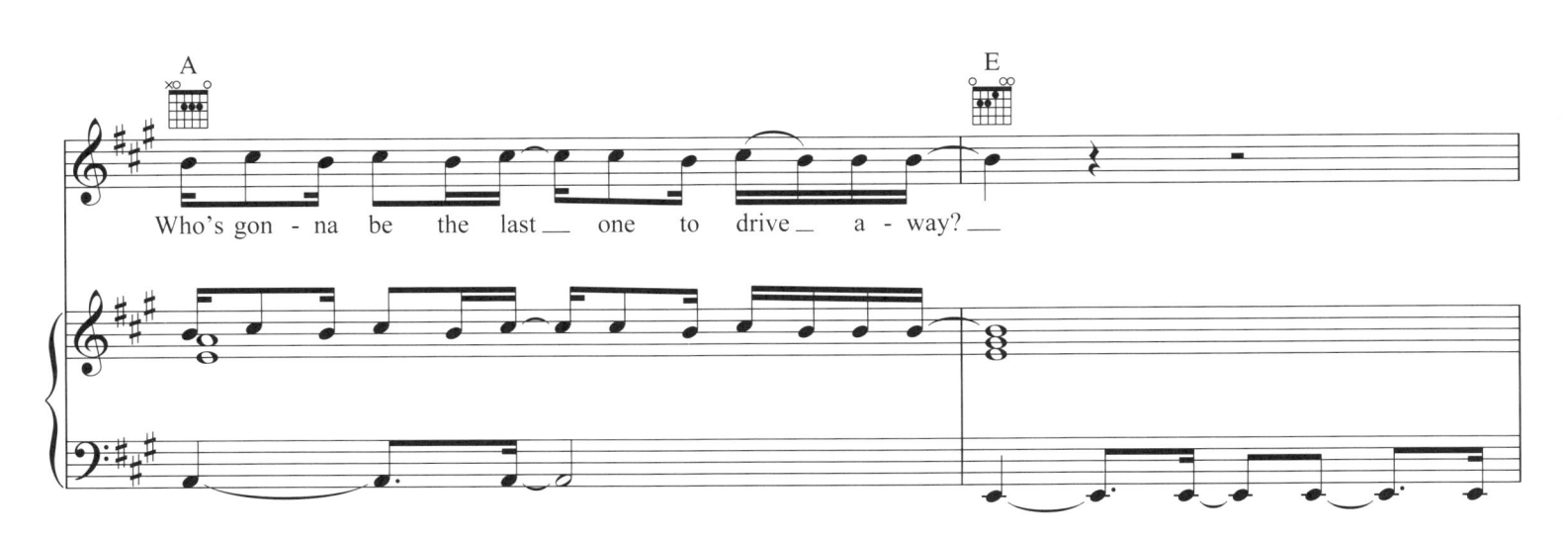

Who's gon-na be the first one to start the fight?

Who's gon-na be the first one to fall a-sleep at night?

Who's gon-na be the last one to drive a-way?

Copyright © 2014 PPM Music Ltd., Holy Cannoli Music, EMI Music Publishing Ltd., BMG Platinum Songs, Music Of Big Deal, Bob Erotik Music and The Family Songbook
All Rights for PPM Music Ltd. Administered by Downtown DMP Songs
All Rights for Holy Cannoli Music Administered by Songs Of Universal, Inc.
All Rights for EMI Music Publishing Ltd. Administered by Sony/ATV Music Publishing LLC, 424 Church Street, Suite 1200, Nashville, TN 37219
All Rights for BMG Platinum Songs, Music Of Big Deal, Bob Erotik Music and The Family Songbook Administered by BMG Rights Management (US) LLC
All Rights Reserved   Used by Permission

72

73

Spac-es be-tween us hold all our se-crets, leaving us speech--less and I don't know why.

Who's gon-na be the first to say good-bye? Ah, ah.

Who's gon-na be the first one to com-pro-mise?

Who's gon-na be the first one to set it all on fire?

Who's gon-na be the last one to drive a-way,

for-get-ting ev-'ry sin-gle prom-ise we ev-er made.

75

A
D
F
ah.
We keep tak - ing turns,
C
G/B
F
C
G/B
oh.
Will we ev - er learn?
Oh,
F
Bm
E
D
D.S. al Coda
when will we learn?
Oh, spac - es be - tween
CODA
A
Who's gon - na be the first to say good - bye?
Ah,

ah.

Who's gon-na be the first to say good-bye? Ah,

The spac-es be-tween us. the spac-es be-tween
Ah,

Repeat and Fade

us.

Optional Ending

The spac-es be-tween us.

STOCKHOLM SYNDROME

Words and Music by HARRY STYLES,
JULIAN BUNETTA, JOHN RYAN
and JOHAN CARLSSON

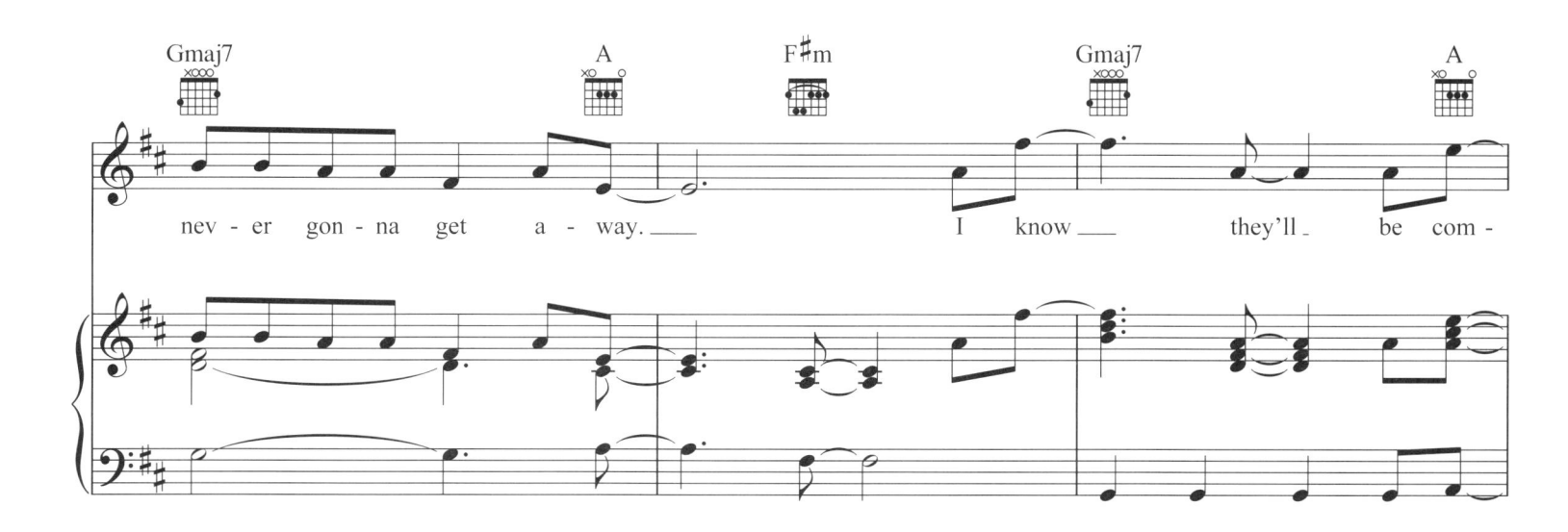

Copyright © 2014 PPM Music Ltd., Holy Cannoli Music, BMG Platinum Songs, Music Of Big Deal, Bob Erotik Music, The Family Songbook and MXM
All Rights for PPM Music Ltd. Administered by Downtown DMP Songs
All Rights for Holy Cannoli Music Administered by Songs Of Universal, Inc.
All Rights for BMG Platinum Songs, Music Of Big Deal, Bob Erotik Music and The Family Songbook Administered by BMG Rights Management (US) LLC
All Rights for MXM Administered by Kobalt Songs Music Publishing
All Rights Reserved   Used by Permission

-ing to find me soon. But I feel I'm get-ting used to being held by you.

Oh baby, look what you've done to me. Oh baby, look what you've done now. Oh baby, I'll never leave if you

Gmaj7
A
N.C.
Gmaj7
keep hold - ing me this way, oh. Oh ba - by,
A
Gmaj7
A
F♯m7
look what you've done to me. Oh ba - by, you've got me tied down.
Gmaj7
A
Gmaj7
Oh ba - by, I'll nev - er leave if you keep hold - ing me this
To Coda
A
D/F♯
Gmaj7
A
way, oh. Who's this man that's hold - ing your hand and

talkin' 'bout your eyes, oh? Used to sing about bein' free but now he's changed his mind. I know they'll be comin' to find me soon. But my Stockholm Syndrome is in your room. Yeah, I fell for you.

All my life I been on my own, oh. I use a light to guide me home, oh. But now together we're alone, oh. And there's no other place I'd ever wanna go. Baby, look what you've done to me.

Gmaj7
A
Gmaj7
Oh ba - by, look what you've done to me. Oh ba - by, ba - by,
A
F♯m
Gmaj7
A
look what you've done now. you've got me tied down.
Oh ba - by, I'll nev - er leave if you
Gmaj7
A
F♯m
Gmaj7
keep hold - ing me this way, oh. Look what
(Lead vocal ad lib.)
Repeat and Fade
Optional Ending
A
Gmaj7
A
F♯m
Gmaj7
you've done to me ba - by.

CLOUDS

Words and Music by LOUIS TOMLINSON,
LIAM PAYNE, ZAYN MALIK,
JULIAN BUNETTA, JAMIE SCOTT
and JOHN RYAN

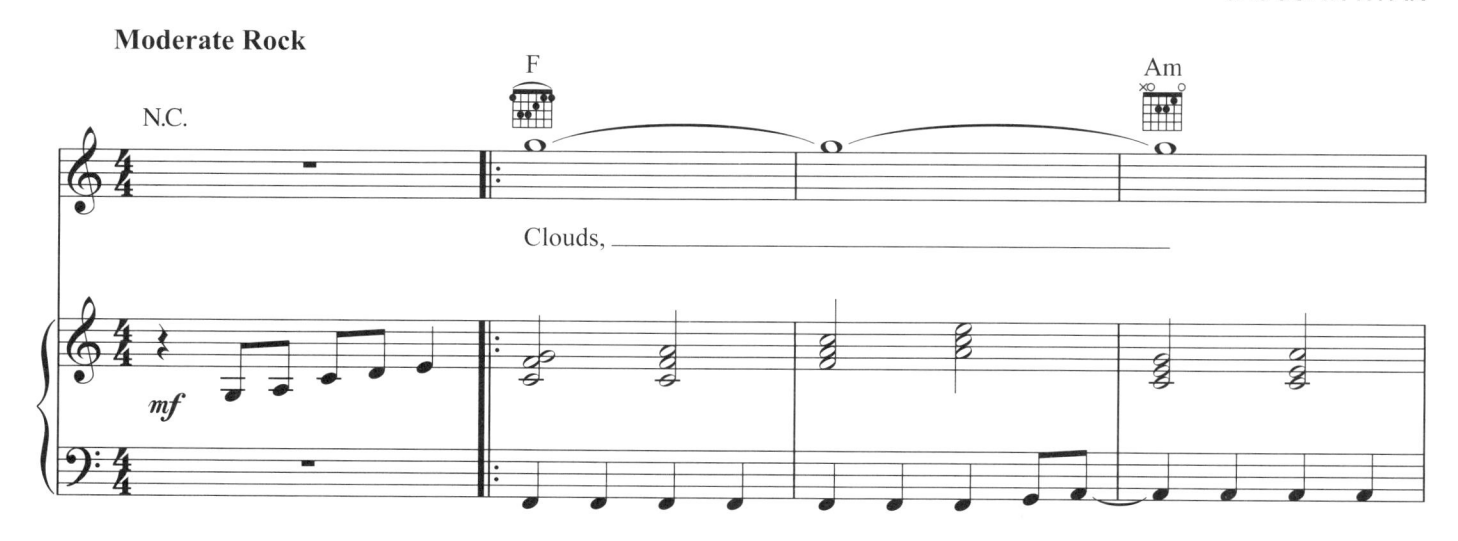

Moderate Rock

Clouds, _____ clouds. _____

I know you say that you don't like it com-pli-cat-ed,
I know you say that you don't like it com-pli-cat-ed,

Copyright © 2014 PPM Music Ltd., Holy Cannoli Music, EMI Music Publishing Ltd., BMG Platinum Songs, Music Of Big Deal, Bob Erotik Music and The Family Songbook
All Rights for PPM Music Ltd. Administered by Downtown DMP Songs
All Rights for Holy Cannoli Music Administered by Songs Of Universal, Inc.
All Rights for EMI Music Publishing Ltd. Administered by Sony/ATV Music Publishing LLC, 424 Church Street, Suite 1200, Nashville, TN 37219
All Rights for BMG Platinum Songs, Music Of Big Deal, Bob Erotik Music and The Family Songbook Administered by BMG Rights Management (US) LLC
All Rights Reserved   Used by Permission

that we should try to keep ___ it sim - ple. But love is nev - er ev -
that you are tired of all ___ the chang - es. But love is al - ways, al -

- er sim - ple, no. _____
- ways chang - in', whoa. _____ Some - day,

you're gon - na see that things ___ that I see. You're gon - na want the air ___

___ that I breathe. You're gon - na wish you nev - er left me.

Here we go a-gain, an-oth-er go a-round for all of my friends. An-oth-er night stopped, will it ev-er end?

Here we go a-gain, an-oth-er go a-round for all of my friends. An-oth-er night stopped, will it

F
C/E
Dm7
ev - er end? We're nev - er com - in' back down. Yeah, we're look - in' down on the
F
Am
clouds, And we go, and we go, and we go
Dm
C/E
F
and we don't stop. Clouds, but we don't,
Am
Dm
C/E
C
no we don't, no we don't ev - er go out. Ah.

ah, ah.

Here we go a-gain, an-oth-er go a-round for all of my friends. An-oth-er night stopped, will it ev-er end?

Play 4 times